D0285884

THE MEAL JESUS GAVE US

The Meal Jesus Gave Us

Tom Wright

WESTMINSTER
JOHN KNOX PRESS
LOUISVILLE · KENTUCKY

First published in Great Britain in 1999
as *Holy Communion for Amateurs*
This edition first published in 2002.

First U.S. edition
Published by Westminster John Knox Press
Louisville, Kentucky

This book is printed on acid-free paper that meets the American National Standards Institute Z39.48 standard. ∞

PRINTED IN THE UNITED STATES OF AMERICA

05 06 07 08 09 10 11 12 — 10 9 8 7 6 5 4 3 2

Library of Congress Cataloging-in-Publication Data

Wright, N. T. (Nicholas Thomas)
  The meal Jesus gave us / Tom Wright.
    p. cm.
  ISBN 0-664-22634-5 (alk. paper)
    1. Lord's Supper I. Title.

  BV825.3.W75 2003
  234'.163—dc21

2003041159

Contents

Foreword . . .

Nothing is more central to Christian practice than the Holy Communion. Yet, curiously enough, little attempt is made to explain it. So many outside the Christian community are just puzzled by it, and many within the church go to Communion from habit but know very little about how it arose and what it means. This is the ideal book for both types of reader. It is written by one of the foremost New Testament scholars in the world, who has the enviable ability to write with engaging charm. It is a book which carries you along with it. You start in shallow water and gradually launch out into the deep meaning of this marvellous 'Jesus meal', as Dr Wright often calls it. The more you know about the New Testament and about the Holy Communion the more you will realise how brilliant this book is, combining simplicity, scholarship and depth. Best of all Dr Wright has written a book which will speak to all types of Christians and unite them over a subject which so often proves divisive. The book flows with apt illustration; the visitor from

Mars, and God's railway, for example, will stay with the reader as windows into what the Holy Communion is all about.

Here is a book that will bring clarity to the enquirer and profound understanding to those who regularly go to Holy Communion. Top academics, too, will find here a skill in communicating the fruits of scholarship in an accessible way that few of them can emulate. I commend this book with all my heart.

Michael Green

Part 1

How it all began

1

The birthday party

You are just sitting down to the table. It is your ten-year-old sister's birthday party. (If you're too old to have a ten-year-old sister, think of your daughter, your niece or your granddaughter.) Everything is ready: the table is laid; the birthday cake is waiting to have its candles lit. There are balloons every-where. People have come with odd-shaped parcels.

Everyone has arrived; but suddenly the doorbell rings. You rush to see who it is. There, just arrived from his own planet, is a polite (and fortunately English-speaking) Martian. He asks graciously if he can come in. This is going to be a birthday party with a difference. You bring him into the house, and to the room where the party is about to start. After the shock and surprise, people realise he's harmless and just wants to enjoy the fun. The party gets under way.

But the Martian, who feels he knows you best since you met him at the door, keeps asking you in a low voice what's going on. Why are all these people here? Why do they pull those things that make a bang? Why are they wearing funny hats? Why does the little girl in the middle of it all keep opening parcels? And why, oh why is someone trying to set fire to that cake?

Every time you try to answer him, it seems to make him more puzzled.

'It's her birthday!'

'You mean she's just been born?'

'No – she was born ten years ago!'

'So what's special about that?'

'We always do this each year.'

'What's a year?'

'It's when . . . well, you know, 365 days.'

'It isn't with us . . . but never mind. Why are they giving her things?'

'Because it's her birthday.'

'Why do you give people things on their birthday?'

'Because we always do . . . I guess – I suppose – I guess it's to tell them we think they're special.'

'Isn't everybody special?'

'Well, yes . . . but on your birthday you're extra special.'

'So why are you wearing those funny hats? Are they special too?'

'Well, yes, in a way . . . they're to make the day different.'

'And why are they setting fire to the cake?'

'They aren't – those are candles.'

'But why are you lighting candles? It's quite light in this room – I can see you perfectly well.'

'We always do . . . I guess it's because it makes the party special again.'

'But why do you put them on the cake?'

4

'I dunno. We just always do. Everybody does.'

'We don't . . . but never mind. Why do you all eat things to celebrate someone's birthday?'

'Now there you've got me. I don't know. But who cares? Here, shut up a minute and have some cake . . .'

Imagine life without parties. Imagine life without the thousand things we do, large and small, that give shape to who we are, that give extra meaning and value to people, to occasions, to the way we do things. I guess you can just about imagine living without any little outward signs as to what you were thinking – no hugs and kisses at the start and end of the day, no wave of the hand, no handshakes, no raising of a glass to toast a bride, or a colleague, or an exam passed. I suppose we might, if we tried very hard, be able to organise our lives without special meals on special occasions, without special trips to special places, without all those things that bring colour and depth to our world. We might just manage it. But life would be very dull.

All human societies, in fact, have developed ways of saying things by doing things. Or, if you like, of meaning things by doing things. A military salute, a pat on the head, the handshake that clinches a business deal: all these are symbolic actions that say things, that mean what they mean within a particular world. And some of the most meaningful things are the special meals that people share together. A wedding reception. The supper when the teenager comes home after six months on the other side of the

5

world. The surprise party to celebrate the end of exams. And, of course, the birthday party.

The birthday party says two things in particular. 'Jane, we wish you a very happy birthday today; and we're glad that, ten years ago, today, you made your grand appearance into the world.' The party joins together the past event and the present moment. (When my children were little, we used to tell a suitably abbreviated version of the story of the day they were born as part of the party entertainment.) It also looks into the future: 'Many happy returns of the day!' we say, even to a ninety-two-year-old. Somehow past, present and future are held together in this one meal. That's why we make it special, with things that are both silly and meaningless at one level (party hats, candles, and so on) and very special and meaningful at another level (they show that this isn't just an ordinary meal, and that while we're enjoying it we aren't just ordinary people, either).

Why do we do all this? Different traditions grow up in different countries, but there seems to be a universal desire to make things special. It's built into us. It's just the way we are. It goes back to some of the oldest stories about the human race: about people who know in their bones that they are made for each other, made to celebrate the good things of life, and made to do all this to the glory of their maker. The person who wrote the book of Genesis would not have needed to ask, like our Martian friend, why we were having a birthday party. It would have made a whole lot of sense.

Now come to a different home. This time you can be the Martian, and tiptoe into a different party.

2

The freedom party

To get into this next party, we will go back in time, and some distance in space. We are in the Jewish quarter of a small town in Turkey in about 200 BC. Like the Martian speaking English, you manage somehow to speak fluent Aramaic (the language most Jews spoke at the time). All day long you have been aware of a growing excitement. People shopping in a hurry. People busily going to and fro. It is spring-time, and there is a sense of something about to happen. Then everything goes quiet in the street. You go over to one of the houses and knock on the door. A girl comes and lets you in, and brings you to the table, where the whole family is gathered.

'What are you all doing?'

'This is one of our special days. We call it Pesach.'

'Pesach? What does that mean?'

'Passing-over. It's what happened when . . . well, you'll see. Listen to the story.'

The older man at the head of the table is starting to speak. Actually, starting to read. He reads in a slightly sing-song voice. It's an old story of the Jewish people, when they were slaves in Egypt.

Everybody seems to know the story; they nod and smile as the tale unfolds.

'We, the people of Abraham, the people called by God to be the light of the world . . . we went down into Egypt, and were slaves there. And our God brought us up from Egypt with a mighty hand and stretched-out arm. He condemned the Egyptians, but he passed over us, and brought us through the Red Sea and into the wilderness; and he gave us his law, and brought us into our promised land.' The story goes on, and on, and on, through all the plagues in Egypt, all the dramatic details.

At one point a little boy, the younger brother of the girl who let you in, pipes up (he seems to be reading, or perhaps his mother is prompting him):

'Why is this night different from all other nights?'

'Because,' says his father, reading still from his text, 'this is the night when our God, the Holy One, blessed be he, came down to Egypt and rescued us from the Egyptians . . .'

'But it isn't,' you whisper to your friend. 'All that happened a long time ago.'

'Yes it is,' the girl whispers back. 'This is the same night. It's like a birthday party. And we are the same people. We are the people of Israel, the people God loved and chose and promised to rescue. We are the people who came out of Egypt.'

'But . . . but . . . not *you*, surely?' you ask. 'It must have been your great-great-great-great grand-parents, with quite a few more "greats".'

'Yes, of course,' she replies. 'But that's not the point. We are not just *us*, if you see what I mean. We are part of *them*, part of the whole of God's people, God's family. We are the same family that came out of Egypt. We are the same family that are having this meal in every Jewish home, everywhere in the world, tonight. This meal makes us all one.'

'But why do you go on doing it? Surely it happened a very long time ago – how can it mean anything for you today?'

'It tells us things about who we are. Things . . . oh, you know, things about God loving us, about God rescuing us. And after all, things are never easy for the Jews, you know. It wasn't just the Egyptians. It was the Babylonians. And then the Persians and the Greeks. (It was after the Greeks ruled us that my family moved here, by the way.) And now we're really worried, because there's a new emperor in the next country, just over the border, where my uncle and aunt live, and he wants to conquer everywhere and make us all his slaves. We're told he specially hates us Jews. So when we celebrate Pesach – Passover – we remind ourselves that we are God's freedom-people. He made us free, and he wants us to be free.'

'So you're saying this meal says all that?'

'Oh yes, all that, but much, much more as well. Actually I find it hard to keep it all in my head, but somehow that doesn't seem to matter . . . what matters is that we're all here, we all belong, we know God loves us, we know he rescued us long

11

ago and he will rescue us again. Oh, Abba's got to the bit I like now . . .'

The older man raises his voice, chanting now with strange, haunting music. He is singing in a language like the one you are talking, only older, stronger, sweeter.

'What's that all about?' you whisper.

'That's when . . .'

All the while you have been eating, and Rebecca (the girl who met you) has explained as you went along what the different things meant. The odd, flat bread had no leaven in it, because the people of Israel had to make their bread without leaven on the night they left Egypt. The bitter herbs (they made you choke and your eyes watered) remind them of the sorrow they had in Egypt. And so on. Even the funny way they sat at table – they didn't sit really, they leaned sideways, 'reclining' they called it – was supposed to say that they were God's free people. Slaves stand; free people recline. The whole meal seemed to say, in a hundred different ways: this is who we are. This is who we were. This is who we will be. And, coming through all of it like the strange music of the story: this is who God was, and is, and will be.

Funny how a meal can do all that. You need the words, of course, but once you get the hang of it it's the meal that somehow says it all, tells it all. And of course by eating the meal you share in the story, God's story, Israel's story. No wonder Jewish family life is so special. No wonder their meals mean so much. And we are now ready to look at a particular

12

Passover meal which came to mean, for some Jews and then for lots of other people as well, more than any other meal in the whole world.

3

The Last Supper
(or was it the first?)

No more disguises. You're going to be a real person
this time. The trick will still work, because no one at
the meal knew what was going on. Except the host,
of course. He had set the whole thing up – arranged
it in secret, because the authorities might have got
wind of it and tried to put a stop to it, or even arrest
him.

He had come into town, and all of you went
along, not just for the ride but because you thought
that This Time It Was Going To Happen. And he
seemed to think so too. He seemed excited, and
strangely troubled as well. He had gone into the
Temple and done something you'd never expected
– attacked the animal-sellers and the money-
changers, stopped the whole system functioning for
a few minutes. It seemed as though he wanted to
say: this whole thing is out of line. It isn't doing
what God wanted it to, and God is going to get rid
of it. But how could he have meant that? What could
he think God would put in its place?

A few nights camping out in the cold spring air at Bethany. Back into the city by day. Jesus teaching crowds, excited crowds, more and more of them as the city got fuller and fuller of pilgrims. All here for the feast, of course: the freedom-party, the kingdom-party. God had set us free from Egypt: now was the time for him to set us free from Rome. And of course you all thought Jesus would be the king who would do it. He would suddenly give the signal, and you would be ready to act – and so would thousands of others. The Roman guards would be nervous. What better time than Passover for the great bid for freedom? Especially with a man of God like Jesus to lead the way.

Passover almost here, and nothing had happened yet. You and the others were wondering what he would do. Then the secret preparations – a day early! What could he have in mind? You were worried this would lead to no good. You'd always had a few doubts as to whether his plan would work out. The authorities had eyes and ears everywhere. But then . . . there you all were round the table, reclining in the time-honoured fashion as God's free people. And the meal began.

'Well, Thomas,' began Simon the hothead, reclining next to you. 'What d'you think he's going to do?'

'I don't know,' you replied. 'I don't see what he *can* do. It's all very well for us to sit here as though it's just another Pesach, but how is all this going to bring in God's kingdom?'

But Jesus was speaking. He was going to say the

16

words the head of the family always said. You knew them by heart; your father had said them year after year. The bread that our fathers ate when they came out of the land of Egypt. The cup to life, the cup to freedom. But ... had you had too much wine, or what? What was that he was saying?

'Take this bread and eat it – it is my body. It's given for you. Do this in remembrance of me.'

The world turned upside down. Everybody was staring. You were convinced he had gone over the top this time. This was the Pesach-meal, the meal that said, you know, the Egypt stuff, the freedom stuff. How could it be about ... Jesus' *body*? And why should we do this 'in remembrance of him'? What could he mean?

You were still buzzing about this when the cup came round. There are so many cups at a Pesach that none of you could remember afterwards which one it was; but you never forgot what happened. Again, the familiar words. Again, Jesus turns them inside out.

'Drink this, all of you: this is my blood of the new covenant. It is shed for you, and for many, so that sins may be forgiven.'

Time to fall through the floor. This was ... too much. His *blood*? Everybody knows Jews don't drink blood. And – *new* covenant? Sins forgiven? Everybody knew, of course, that the prophets had promised that God would eventually make a new covenant with Israel, his people, like when he had brought them out of Egypt. Everybody knew that that would be when he finally forgave Israel's sins once and for all, redeeming them from all their troubles, giving them freedom. Yes, that was what Passover was pointing forward to. But somehow the future seemed to have arrived in the present, and there you were, sleepy with food and wine, quite unready for it. And how on earth could all this have anything to do with Jesus' . . . *blood*?

Heads spinning, you went out into the night. Then it all happened. Asleep in the garden; why haven't we gone back to Bethany as usual? Jesus off with his three closest friends, though you can't hear what they're saying. Then the soldiers, the torches, the arrest. All you can remember is running, running, off into the dark, tearing the hem of your cloak on the branch of an olive-tree, with your heart pounding and an odd jumble of Jesus' words going round like a nightmare in your head. Bread and cup. Body and blood. Death and remembering.

Then the Friday, hiding like a rat in a hole.

Then the news. The worst. The end. The shame. All your fears come true, all your doubts confirmed. And in the middle of it all a meal that should have been a Passover but hadn't been, with words that should have pointed to God's great new redemption but obviously didn't, said by the one who should have been Israel's Messiah but who now obviously wasn't.

4

New meal, new family

One more scene, and then we'll stop play-acting. This, though, is where the story really starts, so we're going to go into it a little more deeply, and take three chapters over it. We're going back to Turkey, to a little town a hundred miles from the east coast, under the shadow of the Taurus Mountains. The year is AD 56. And this time I am going to be the character in the story. Why should you have all the fun?

Let's set the scene. The first day of the working week. Everybody up and doing, shops open, bread baked, workshops busy. But a few of us have already been up for an hour or two. We've been over in Philemon's house, the big one at the end of the street. What have we been doing? Yes, I know the neighbours have been gossiping. Don't believe everything you hear at the barber's. I guess I have to start a little way back.

A couple of years ago, a fellow from our town went on business to the big city down at the coast. There he met a strange fellow, a Jew with an attitude, a Jew with a difference. He was in prison, actually, but that hadn't stopped him telling our old friend Epaphras a story that changed his life. He brought the story back here, and it's changed our lives too, I can tell you.

The story is so strange, and yet when people tell it it does things to you. Warms you inside, like a hot drink on a cold day. Makes you sorry and glad and eager and quiet all at once. Makes you look at everything differently. What's with these Jews? I'm not sure I know, but if this story is typical of their stuff they've certainly got something.

Of course, we know a bit about the Jews. There's a synagogue in the town, though not a very big one, and people know the Jews keep special holidays (including a lazy day at the end of every week! Nice work if you can get it). Rumour has it they do strange things to their baby boys, too, but in a family context I won't say more. Oh, and they won't eat meat. Or perhaps it's just that they don't eat pork, which is what we mostly get in the market. And of course, as everyone knows, they don't worship the gods (that's why most people call them atheists). Somehow the gods don't seem to mind too much, although word is that the Jews have a rough time of it. Some folk say they ask for it, some say no, they're just being loyal to their own god and you can't blame them for that. But the rest of us, we don't think too much about them.

Let me tell you how it used to be for us. We went to our own gods, of course, in their temples; gods of harvest if we were planting crops, gods of love if we were getting married, gods of commerce if we were doing business. You name it, we had a god for it. You had to keep them sweet. And on their special days – well, of course, we had a party. Went to their temple, gave the priest an animal to sacrifice, and then went round the back to the restaurant and pigged out good and proper. I won't say we never got blind drunk, and I won't say we didn't do some pretty strange things when we were all under the influence, especially as there were the usual girls and boys who sort of hung around offering their services. I guess the priests made a bit on the side that way too. It was all part of the deal.

Anyway, as I was saying, Epaphras came back and told us this story. The story of a Jew called Jesus. He was what the Jews called the 'Messiah', a sort of king – at least, his friends thought he was, but the Romans got him and crucified him (I could have told them that's what the Romans would do to a rebel king) and that seemed the end of it. But then – this is the bit that made me go weak at the knees when I heard it – a couple of days later, on the first day of the week, there he was alive again. Not just staggering around as though he hadn't really died, but alive in a new sort of way. Nobody could explain it and I certainly can't, but somehow it seems to make so much sense despite everything . . . And the Jews believe that their Messiah, when he comes, will be the Lord of the whole world. Yes, us too! Can you believe it? Me, bow down to a Jewish king? Must be crazy. Or so I thought to begin with.

Anyway, hearing this gave me such a start, it was as though I'd been asleep and suddenly woken up.

Or as though I'd just been trundling along minding my own business and suddenly fallen head over heels in love. Or been watching the telly in black and white and suddenly it came through in colour (yes, I know we haven't invented it yet, but *you* will know what I mean).

And now . . . well, here we are. We're like a new family. And of course the thing about families is that they eat together . . .

5

New meal, new story

So, like I said, it's as though we're now a single family. Thirty-two of us who heard the story and had the same thing happen to us. My wife heard the story and it had the same effect on her, too, but half the others are people we'd never really thought of as our type before. Slaves, too, quite a few of them. And you know what? We share things round. We treat each other as brothers and sisters (weird! But it seems to work). It's called *agape*, which is like what we used to mean by 'love', but somehow it's more . . . well, *practical*. It means you do things differently. Everybody counts.

And of course we don't go to the temples any more. No; you see, when we heard the story it was as though everything we thought we knew about the gods sort of crumpled up in a little heap, and we found we were getting to know another god . . . perhaps I should say, God. The more we heard about that Jesus, the more this God seemed to come to us, to welcome us. And (I know this is going to sound really odd, but believe me, it's the way it feels), we find we, well, sort of *know* him. The God of the Jews, I guess. Explains why they stuck to him all those years. Quite a character. And he seems to know us pretty well, too. And all those things we used to do, all the things we used to get up to with those other gods, that made us feel dirty or petty or cheap or mean . . . well, he knows about all that, too, but somehow he's made it all right. It's all to do with this story about Jesus – and about why he died . . .

Oh yes, sorry, I'm getting carried away. You want to know why we were up at the crack of dawn on the first day of the week, even before the baker started his oven up. Well, it's another of those Jewish things. They have this meal which they share together. Passover, it's called. It's a story of theirs from way, way back, about the time when their God – yes, this God we're getting to know – rescued them from Egypt. That was fine, but things never went right for them for too long, and he promised them that he would set them free in a new way one day. That he would do a new thing – deal with their problems once for all, and in the process call the whole world to be his people! Can you imagine it – the God of the Jews wanting us all to be his family? Well, the Jews always said their God was the creator of the world, so maybe it makes sense. And of course if their King is the Lord of the whole world, there we are. (Sorry, yes, I know we shouldn't say that so loud. 'Our Lord and Saviour' has eyes and ears all over the place. But – here, let me whisper it – *if you ask me, Jesus is the real 'Lord and Saviour'. Caesar, with all those new temples and statues, is just a sham.*)

So, where were we? Oh yes, the Jews have this

Passover meal. And when Jesus was about to be arrested and handed over to the Romans, he had a Passover meal with his followers. But he changed it. Now it was all about God doing what he'd promised in that new way. Somehow Jesus was going to die – he seems to have known that – and he said that they should repeat this meal in memory of him. Heavy stuff? But that's not the half of it. He took the bread and said, 'This is my body.' And he took the wine and said, 'This is my blood.' Shivers down my spine! I mean, when we used to go to the temples up the street we thought we were sharing in the body and blood of the god when we had that binge round the back. That's why it gave us such good vibes (never lasted, mind you).

So, well, this is where the story really starts: every first weekday the whole family gets together. Has to be early so folk can get off to work straight after – specially the slaves, of course. And we don't have a real meal: that gets expensive, and then you get into questions about who pays and how much people eat and drink, and the whole point of it is that we're doing this all together as a family. We sort out who needs what and how much we all give to the family at other times, but this time is too special to raise questions like that. Epaphras said his friend in prison had run into difficulties with some of the family in Greece over stuff like that. Well, Corinth always was a funny old place, if you ask me.

The great thing is that – well, here's the punch line and I hardly know how to say it! – when we break and eat the bread together, and drink the wine together, it's like the best moment we ever had in the old temples but in a different dimension altogether. No, that's not the place to start. It's like we were there, really there, when he had that last supper with his friends. Yes: there we are, in Philemon's house, first thing on a Sunday morning, with the town about to wake up all around us and get off to work, and I could swear Jesus himself is there with us. And he loves us. And we love him. And because of that we really love each other – yes, even funny Philemon with his stuck-up ways, and that runaway slave of his, Onesimus, who came back after meeting this Jewish jailbird. And this God – this Jewish God, who made the whole world, not like our cheap little tinpot gods – is there with us, like a mother looking after a family of little babies. Perhaps like a mother bird brooding over her chicks. Well, you know what I mean . . . or perhaps you don't?

6

New meal, new life

And of course there's something else. Part of the story is that this God is taking the world somewhere. He's got plans. Apparently he's promised to do for all of us what he did for Jesus after he died. And for the whole world too. Yes, that really blows me away. This God really does love the whole world, and wants to make it all alive in a new way, like he did with Jesus on the first day of the week, all of forty or more years ago. And when he does that we'll meet Jesus himself! He'll be there. He'll come back to us – or maybe I should say we'll be there with him; I don't really know how it'll be or what words to use. But this is the point: when we take the bread and break it and eat it, when we take the wine and share it around, it isn't only that we seem to be there with him at his last supper. We are there with him in his new world. What we do seems to bring all the past – all the story of Jesus – and all the future – the time when he comes back again, when God makes the whole world new – all together into one moment. Apparently the Jews used to say this about their Passover meals, or something like it.

I suppose it's like a birthday party, really, remembering the birth and saying 'many happy returns' all at the same time. Jesus' birthday party? No, I suppose in a sense it's our birthday party. Anyway, we do it every week, because every Sunday reminds us of the day he rose again from the dead. We call it 'the Lord's day', you know. And that meant that his death wasn't a failure, as everyone thought; it was his victory. He faced death and beat it. He took the worst the world could do and came out on top. And somehow in the middle of that he took everything we've done – all that stuff *I* used to get into, I won't mention *you* – and did away with it. And when we eat the bread and drink from that cup, that's what we celebrate. Forgiveness. It's amazing. And each time we do it I have the strangest sense . . . that somehow doing it says it, that somehow doing it shouts it to the world around. I feel all those old gods cowering in a corner. They don't like it. They know they've met their match. Sometimes they try to hit back at us (I gather the Jew in prison had a rough time of it when lots of folk started turning their back on the old gods). But whatever they do to us, even if things get really bad, earthquakes or violence or whatever, he's with us. It'll be all right. And more than all right.

Oh, and one more thing. This is really strange. Of course, when you've been doing what we used to do for as long as we used to do it – yes, the old temples and all that stuff – it's a habit that dies hard. But somehow when you've been at one of these meals it seems the whole world's a different place. You don't want to go and get drunk or fool around with those girls and boys. And you don't want to go out and cheat in business, either, or take bribes, or treat the poor like dirt the way we used to. It's as though – well, it's a bit like when we used to think we were eating and drinking the god, but actually it's quite different as well – it's as though Jesus himself is somehow now living in us. Scary, huh? You'd better believe it. And it's not that he's a bully or beats us up with a big stick if we don't do what he wants. It's more as though he loves us so much that we just want to be like him, to do things his way. And it's as though he's put his breath inside us. The Jews apparently talk about God's breath, or God's wind. I begin to see what they mean.

How do we know what Jesus' way is? Well, partly we just sense this breath, this spirit, leading us, nudging us, one way rather than another. But that's not all. Every time we have this meal we get one of the folks who can read to tell us again one of the stories Jesus' friends wrote about him after his death. He said so many things that are so different, and yet they make so much sense. Who wrote them all down? I can't remember the name – began with a Q, I think. Or maybe I dreamt that. But that's not the point. Everything he said was like another little sip from that great story, the story that changed me and goes on changing me. It all just fits together. The story, the meal, the God of the Jews, this strange new family. And me in the middle feeling like a new man. The whole bit.

29

What do we call it, this meal? Well, we don't have a real name for it. We just do it. We just say we're going to break bread. 'The breadbreaking', I suppose you could call it. But we do sometimes call it 'the sharing' – sharing with Jesus, sharing with each other. And we do sometimes call it 'the thank-you meal', because whenever Jesus had meals with his friends he began by saying 'thank you' to this God. And one of the Jews in town who's joined the family calls it 'the Lord's feast'. But it doesn't much matter what we call it. It's just . . . well, I feel it's the thing which binds us together. And it gives me strength to go on every week, to pray, to live differently, to discover this God all over the place. What's that? You'd like to come next week? Well, I'll let Philemon know. See you there.

Part 2

The thank-you party

7

Putting the story together today

So what happens when we sit back and try to put this whole story together today?

Many people today, including many Christians, don't realise where the central Christian act came from, or what it meant to begin with. Lots of people, including lots of scholars – theologians, historians and others – have argued about the details. Some of these details are important, and questions will always remain. But the basic fact of the matter is this: what Christians do today when they meet to break bread and drink wine together is the central Christian action, which links us in an unbroken line to that little church in Turkey nineteen hundred and some years ago, and ultimately of course to Jesus and his friends in the Upper Room on the night he was about to be betrayed (and denied, forsaken, arrested, tried, mocked and executed). And it links us, too, to almost all Christians throughout the world today ('almost' because there are some, like the Salvation

Army, who for various reasons do not celebrate this meal).

The question for us must be: how can we, today, get in on this story? How can we understand this remarkable gift of God and use it properly? How can we make the best of it?

Why has this special meal become so controversial? Why do people argue about its meaning, and how best to celebrate it – and even what to call it? That'll be in this chapter and the next one (Chapters 7 and 8).

Let's begin with the difficult bit. Why is this meal, or symbolic meal, so controversial?

Actually, once you understand how symbolic actions work, you shouldn't be surprised. A footballer in Glasgow once nearly started a riot by pretending to play a flute. Why? His club was associated with Scottish and Irish Protestants, some of whom still march through the streets playing flutes to celebrate a Protestant victory over Roman Catholics several hundred years ago. The other team, and their supporters, were traditionally Roman Catholics. Symbols are so powerful that they can be threatening. (Of course, the Roman Catholic community have their provocative symbols as well.)

Symbols sum up, in one little action or word, a whole way of life that makes some people feel happy and at home and other people feel as though there's a knife in their ribs. And when a symbol or symbolic action is not fully explained – and it's always difficult to explain a symbol – then sometimes people can get the wrong end of the stick and feel they are being squeezed out or threatened.

Sadly, that's what has happened with this meal. Yes, the meal that should declare, every time, that all Christians belong together has come to be, often enough, a sign of our disunity. The newspapers love to get hold of scandals in the Church – some wretched minister caught with his trousers down or his hand in the till – but the real scandal goes on every week whenever the Jesus-meal is a sign, not of Christian unity, but of division. And, tragically, that old Protestant–Catholic split has been, in the Western world at least, the main fault line. People are marked out, or marked down even, by how they celebrate Jesus' party. Even by what they call it.

Let's begin with that question, since otherwise we won't know how to talk about it. Our early Christian friend had four phrases. The first, you remember, was simply 'the breadbreaking'. The early Christians in Acts met together 'to break bread', and presumably this doesn't mean simply 'to eat together'. This was the breadbreaking which spoke of Jesus and his death.

The second phrase was 'the sharing', which is the English translation of a Greek word you may have heard, *koinonia*. Another translation of that same word is 'communion', which means that we are communing, or sharing, in the death and risen life of Jesus (as well as communing with one another as we do so). Because we 'commune' with one another in a variety of ways, when we use this word to describe this service we often add the word 'holy', meaning 'special', 'set apart for God': hence, 'Holy Communion'.

The third name was 'the thank-you meal'. Jesus always said 'thank you' to God; the Church, in breaking the bread and pouring out the wine, says 'thank you' to God for what he did in Jesus. The Greek for 'thank you' is *eucharisto* (perhaps you've heard modern Greeks say this, pronounced *efaristo*), and some of the earliest Christians therefore called the meal 'the Eucharist'. This is perhaps the most common word for the meal in use among Christians around the world today.

The fourth name was 'the Lord's Meal', or 'the Lord's Supper'. 'Supper' sounds rather strange in some ways today, because that English word now normally refers to an *evening* meal, whereas this meal was and is celebrated, often enough, first thing in the morning. However, since Jesus' original meal was an evening one, and our Jesus-meals look back to that event, it has its own point to make.

A fifth name didn't come into use until a bit later. When Christianity reached Rome, and when the meal became regularly celebrated in the Latin language (most Christians in Rome spoke Greek as their first language until well into the second century at least), the end of the meal would be signalled by the person presiding saying, 'Go – you are sent out'. This, as we shall see, is a powerful part of the whole event, as those who have fed upon the death and risen life of King Jesus are equipped to serve him in the world. The Latin for this phrase is *'ite – missa est'*. From this there developed the word 'Mass', the meal that ends with this sending-out, this commissioning.

Each of these words now carries all sorts of other meanings as well, through their use in different strands and branches of Christianity down the centuries. It is these different uses, and the different theories and ideas that have sprung up around them, that have often caused controversy, and, tragically, bitterness and division at the very point where Christians should be most united. That's what we have to explore further in the next chapter.

8

The party and the parties

The Jesus-meal (to use an unusual though neutral phrase for it) was already woven into the heart of Christian living by the time Paul wrote to Corinth in the mid-50s, twenty years or so after Jesus' death and resurrection. It held such a strong place in Paul's own thinking that he could speak of the very action of the meal as 'proclaiming the death of the Lord until he comes'. *Doing* it *said* it.

Touch this symbol, then, and you touch a nerve centre.

In the first few hundred years of the Church, Communion/Eucharist/Supper/Mass was celebrated regularly, and various theories grew up about it. Early in the second century Ignatius, Bishop of Antioch and one of the first developers of Paul's thought, refers to it as 'the medicine of immortality'. Around the same time, the book called *Didache* ('Teaching') explains how to say the prayer over the bread and the wine. People didn't feel tied slavishly to the exact words Jesus used at the Last Supper.

By later in the second century, as Christianity made its way within the Roman world, Christians saw the Jesus-meal taking the place, roughly speaking, of their former pagan religious meals. Paul already borrows language from the pagan cult-meals to describe what happens in the Lord's Meal.

Simultaneously, many Christian leaders, aware of their Jewish heritage, were seeking to use Jewish language and imagery to describe their Christian life and work. Over against some anti-Jewish teachers, the mainstream Church emphasised that they were not a 'new' family, but rather the worldwide extension of the Old Testament people of God. The Jewish story was the beginning of the Christian story.

For these and other reasons, the office-bearers who played host at the Lord's Meal began to be described as 'priests'. Those who used this language knew that Christian ministers weren't like either pagan or Jewish priests. Christians, after all, didn't sacrifice animals. But office-bearers in the early Church came quite soon to be described, metaphorically to begin with, as 'priests' offering a 'sacrifice', even though everybody knew they weren't really. It was just a manner of speaking, a natural way of talking about leading worship. (Confusingly, the English word 'priest' comes from the Greek *presbyteros* and the Latin *presbyter*, which simply mean 'elder'.)

There is a time and place for a full history of the Jesus-meal, and this isn't it. Enough to say that over the next thousand years or so the 'priest' became the familiar figure in the local church, and for much of Christendom it was assumed that one of his main functions was to offer what came to be called 'the sacrifice of the Mass'. The bread and wine became Jesus' body and blood. Learned theories were developed to explain what this meant; for most ordinary worshippers it was simply a miracle that the priest performed, which they depended on for God's grace, forgiveness and salvation. Priests were powerful.

For all sorts of reasons many people in the Western world came to see that this simply wouldn't do. It wasn't true to Jesus, to the early Church, to the New Testament. The Reformation in the sixteenth century, led by people like Martin Luther and John Calvin in Europe, John Knox in Scotland, and William Tyndale and Thomas Cranmer in England, insisted in their different ways on reforms designed to bring Christianity back on course with Jesus and the New Testament. They had, of course, their own agendas and mixed motives. They didn't always agree with each other. But they agreed, broadly, on the following things.

The Bible must be read in one's own language. Worship, too, particularly the central act, must be in the tongue of the people. Being a Christian was basically a matter of trusting God, not trying to earn his favour with 'good works'; God had already done everything we needed for salvation, once and for all, in Jesus ('justification by faith'). Christians didn't go to 'Purgatory' when they died; they didn't need endless 'Masses' for their souls. Christians were equal in God's sight; the clergy were just people with a particular job. All this, and more, came as a package deal.

In the middle was the Jesus-meal. It wasn't a bit of clerical mumbo-jumbo. You didn't need it to get out of Purgatory. It wasn't a good deed that you 'did' (or that the clergy did) to earn God's favour. It couldn't be a sacrifice, because Jesus died once for all. To treat the bread and wine as Jesus' body and blood was idolatry (see Chapter 12). People needed to hear the Bible and understand it, to have God's grace at work in their hearts by faith, to return to the simplicity of the early Church. The Church, the priests and the Pope had become too rich, powerful and worldly. A great many who remained Roman Catholics heartily agreed, as St Francis would have done centuries before.

For the reforms to work, there had to be political change. Religion wasn't a private matter (that was an eighteenth-century novelty); it affected all society. Huge social and cultural changes swept Europe. The divide between Catholic and Protestant, between 'Mass' and 'Communion', came to symbolise deep-level differences between communities. Both sides burnt people at the stake for believing the wrong things. Wars were fought. Then, as with a huge and horrible family row, it seemed for a long time that nothing could be said or done. Both sides sulked, remembering atrocities, fearful of giving an inch lest 'they' take a mile.

That, unfortunately, is the atmosphere in which, to this day, many Christians celebrate the Jesus-meal, the family-meal, the meal that ought to declare to the wider world that there is one God, one Lord, one Spirit. Is it too much to hope that in the new millennium we might discover how to heal the family wounds?

9

Living in God's time

The hardest thing to grasp with sacraments is that they invite us to look at *time* in a different way. Think of it like this.

Supposing you're a teenager at school. (If you're not, you can imagine it.) Think about your schooldays, from the very first day you went to school right through to the day, still in the future, when you will finally leave and go out into the wider world. See this time like a railway line, with a beginning, a middle and an end. You're somewhere in the middle. (No doubt the train seems to be taking forever to get where it's going.)

Think back to the beginning. It was exciting, and a little scary. You had new clothes and shoes. A shiny new schoolbag, with sharp pencils, a ruler, perhaps a brand new notebook. Everything about the day said that it was a new beginning. You were becoming a new person.

Think on to the end. One day you will leave school, hopefully with some qualifications to help you to move forward into your new life. After ten, twelve, maybe even fourteen years you'll reach the destination.

And what about now? Today, or next Monday, may seem like just another boring old schoolday. You're halfway along the track, and it seems miles from the excitement of the first day or the drama of the last one. But the present moment is held in place by those two days. You are doing what you are doing today because you are the person who began in that way, and who will end in that way. Memories can be re-activated; the past can catch up with you. Hopes, too, can be life-changing: the future can come to meet you. Past and future give meaning to the present.

This is the tricky bit. Christians believe that in Jesus *God's future came rushing into the present to meet us*. It isn't just that we were chugging along a railway line, steadily moving towards a distant destination. At one particular moment we discovered *another train coming to meet us from that destination*. At the heart of the New Testament is the claim that God unveiled his secret plan for the world in the person of Jesus himself, and supremely in his death and resurrection. Jesus announced that 'the kingdom of God' was bursting into the present moment. It didn't look like what people had expected. Indeed, to some people it felt more like a train rushing towards them on the same track, crashing into them, and smashing their hopes to bits. But when hope put itself together again on Easter morning it became clear that this really was what God had had in mind all along. And that's where Christianity began. That moment is the one we now look back to as the start of it all. Get it?

God's *future* came into the *present* in Jesus, and so has become part of our *past*.

And if in one sense God's future comes to meet us in the present, in another sense God's past comes to catch us up. Every time we stop in a station on the way an express comes from our original starting-point, at the speed of light, to be present to us, to remind us where we've come from. Precisely because the vital event in our *past* always was part of God's *future*, it has no difficulty in catching up again and again with our ever-changing *present*. (I know this is getting complicated. If you can think of a better way of putting it, good luck to you.) As we are travelling the line that leads from the Upper Room to the great feast in God's new world, from the victory of Calvary and Easter to the final victory over death itself (1 Corinthians 15:26), *we find at every station* – in other words, at every celebration of the Jesus-meal – *that God's past catches up with us again, and God's future comes to meet us once more.*

All of this is summed up in a brilliant little sentence in 1 Corinthians 11:26. 'Whenever you eat this bread and drink this cup,' says Paul, 'you announce the Lord's death until he comes.' The present moment ('whenever') somehow holds together the one-off past event ('the Lord's death') and the great future when God's world will be remade under Jesus' loving rule ('until he comes'). Past and future come rushing together into the present, pouring an ocean of meaning into the little bottle of 'now'.

What does this mean for the questions and

puzzles that have become such flag-waving matters in the Church?

10

Jesus' death then and now

How many times are you going to die?

Silly question, you will say: once, of course. Then again ... perhaps not. After all, many religions have supposed that after death all creatures are reincarnated in another form. You might come back as a frog, or a cow. An elephant might come back as a royal baby. And so on. And of course they would then have to die again. And again, and again. Reincarnation has become popular again in recent years, as a glance at the bookshops will reveal.

The Jews didn't believe this. They believed that people died once and once only. By Jesus' day they had developed various beliefs about the afterlife, but they never imagined that life went round in cycles, with people being born and dying over and over again. Birth, life and death went in a line, not round in a ring.

The Reformers' protest against what they saw as mediaeval Catholic distortions of Christianity was, at its heart, an insistence on the Jewish straight-line view of life and death over against a circular one, as applied specifically to Jesus. They objected to the belief (which wasn't necessarily official Catholic teaching, but was clearly what lots of people believed) that Jesus had to be crucified again in every Mass. The bread became literally his body; it was broken, indicating his death; the sacrifice had taken place. The priest had done something which extracted favour and forgiveness from God. He therefore did it on an 'altar', sometimes made of stone, and wore 'sacrificial' robes.

Against this, the Reformers emphasised three closely linked things. This chapter is about (1) and (2); we shall come to (3) presently. (1) Nothing we do can earn God's forgiveness and favour. It remains a free gift. (2) God's gift is based on Jesus' once-for-all sacrifice, which can't and needn't be repeated. (3) Jesus is not physically present in the bread. They therefore replaced the 'altar' with a table, and got rid of sacrificial robes. What clergy wear, and what they call the object they break bread on, still has a symbolic meaning for many people in churches, even if they couldn't tell you why.

The Reformers were right to insist that Christianity adopts the straight-line view of time as opposed to the circular view. What God has done in Jesus is done for all time. Any suggestion that each Jesus-meal is doing something fresh, an action of our own, is wrong. In any case, to suppose that a sacrifice is something humans do to earn God's favour is unbiblical. That's how pagan sacrifices may have worked. Some Jews may have mistakenly thought of their own sacrifices in that light, though it's difficult to be sure. But in the Bible sacrifices were not human 'good works' designed to amass merit, to earn heavenly brownie points. They were the God-given means of establishing and maintaining fellowship between God and his people.

We mustn't forget what we said in the last chapter about God's railway-system, God's scheme of time. Jesus' death and resurrection were God's future arriving in the present, becoming the crucial past event for all moments and events thereafter. As one New Testament book puts it very daringly, because the cross reveals the true loving heart of God, we can speak of Jesus as 'the Lamb slain from the foundation of the world' (Revelation 13:8). The truth of Calvary is, in that sense, present to all times and all places, even though it had to happen once, uniquely and climactically.

So whenever we celebrate the Jesus-meal we discover that Jesus' death, the unique past event, somehow catches up with us again. We don't, of course, sacrifice Jesus afresh. But when sacrifice was offered, in the Jewish temple or the pagan ones, the result was a feast. And every Jesus-meal is a feast – on the one, single sacrifice.

But if we don't sacrifice Jesus afresh, nor do we offer a *different* sacrifice. The Reformers, eager to stress that we weren't sacrificing Jesus, sometimes spoke (it's in some regular Communion prayers) about offering God 'a sacrifice of praise and thanksgiving'. To some this has looked as though the Reformers were doing what they were accusing the Catholics of: offering a different sacrifice to the one, complete, perfect sacrifice of Jesus. Sacrifices of thanksgiving are of course thoroughly biblical (Hebrews 13:15–16); they aren't designed to *earn* God's favour, but precisely to thank God for it.

The Jesus-meal therefore brings together sacrifice, feast and thanksgiving. The one, unrepeatable sacrifice has caught up with us wherever we stop on our forward journey. The feast belongs with that one sacrifice, and only makes sense insofar as it goes with it. The thanksgiving is our appropriate gratitude for unearned grace. Once you understand this, a lot of the prayers we use in the Jesus-meal will start to make sense.

In particular, you may grasp the meaning of the strange phrase 'do this *in remembrance of me*'. That doesn't just mean 'remembering' Jesus and his death. We do not simply recall the events of Calvary with our minds and hearts in faith, and love, and awe – though we should certainly do that every time we come to Jesus' table. It means that somehow Jesus is present; that his one-off death is made contemporary with us. The unique past event rushes forward to accompany us on our journey.

But how then *is* Jesus 'present'? In order to answer that, we must look first at how the Jesus-meal points forward. We show forth the Lord's death, says Paul, 'until he comes'.

11

A taste of what's to come

When the Israelites were wandering through the desert on their way to the promised land, Moses sent spies ahead into Canaan who would come back to tell what they had seen. (You can read the story in Numbers 13.)

It was a disaster. Out of the twelve spies who went, one from each tribe, ten lost heart. 'The people are strong,' they said. 'They're huge – they've got giants there. We felt like grasshoppers. Their cities are fortified. There's no way we can take the place.' Only two of the spies, Caleb and Joshua, disagreed. But the people, hearing the news, refused to go up and attack the land. God sent them instead on a roundabout route through the desert until the entire generation had died, leaving only Joshua and Caleb to enter the land of promise.

But in the middle of that sad story there was a sign of hope. The spies came to a dry stream-bed where there were grapes growing – huge grapes, so heavy that a branch with a single cluster needed two of them to carry it. They called the place Cluster Brook, in Hebrew *Wadi Eshcol*. They brought pomegranates and figs as well. Even fruit from the land of promise didn't convince the rest of the Israelites. But as the story was told that fruit became an important symbol of hope. One day they would get there, and there would be enough clusters for everybody.

Take that image and weave it together with the picture from the last two chapters, of the train rushing forward to meet you from your destination. God's future, as we saw, has arrived in the present in the person of Jesus of Nazareth, and in his death and resurrection in particular. In him we see a glimpse of what God's new world is to be like. In his resurrection, in particular, we already have a foretaste of the new world, in which not only human bodies but the whole cosmic order will be transformed to share in the freedom which goes with the glory that God will shower upon his people (Romans 8:18–30). Paul, writing about this glorious future hope, uses the language of the wilderness wanderings of Israel to make the point.

Some people think of the Christian's 'promised land' as simply 'heaven'. Some even think that this could be rather boring. How wrong they are. In Paul's writings, the Christian's 'promised land' is the entire renewed world. If we die before the time, we will go to 'heaven', that is, into God's dimension of existence. But the long-term hope is that all those in 'heaven' and presently on earth will be transformed, re-embodied, to join in the new life when (as Revelation 21 says, echoing an old Jewish theme) God will make new heavens and a new earth. Within this transformation of reality, Jesus himself will be personally present. Every longing of our hearts will be satisfied in our meeting with him and being nourished by his presence and his love. Sometimes the New Testament talks of this event as Jesus' 'coming'; sometimes of his 'royal presence'. These are different ways of saying something for which we don't have the right language at the moment, but which will be real, solid and lovely when it happens.

If that is our promised land, what are the grapes which the spies bring back to us? Many things, no doubt. The Holy Spirit is spoken of in the New Testament as the 'down-payment' or 'guarantee' of our inheritance. Paul writes movingly about the way in which, though faith and hope will be no longer necessary for those whose journey is over, love will simply go on for ever. Jesus himself is the one who has come rushing forward in person from God's future to meet us, to die for us, in our own time, within history.

Put these together, turn them into a symbolic action (and remember, once again, that symbolic actions are among the most powerful things in the world) and what do you have? Why, the food and drink which we can eat in the present but which is brought forward to us from the future: the food and drink which we share in love with one another; the food and drink over which we pray for the Spirit to come from God's future to transform our present; the food and drink which speak uniquely of the presence and love, the death and resurrection, of Jesus himself. In other words, of course, the bread and the wine that we share in the Jesus-meal. Holy Communion, the Eucharist, the Lord's Supper, the Mass, the Breaking of Bread – this meal gains part of its deepest meaning from God's future as much as from God's past.

This is our equivalent of the grapes of Eshcol, the food from Cluster Brook that tells us where our destination is, even if the fainthearted don't want to know about it. This is the food which will assure us that we are on the right road, and that the God who began a good work in us, and now feeds us with his own life, the life of his own Son, will bring that good work to completion when all things are made new and we stand at last in the presence of Jesus himself. This meal is designed by the Father, by Jesus, by the Holy Spirit, to bring a taste of things to come, fresh grapes from the land of promise for those at present wandering in the dusty desert.

'As often as you eat this bread,' said Paul, 'and drink this cup, you announce the Lord's death until he comes.' Held secure between past and future – God's past, God's future – we go forward on our journey strengthened and given hope. And between faith and hope we are given love, because we are given Jesus' own presence.

12

The presence of Jesus

Let's do the fly-on-the-wall trick again.

Two men are sitting in a castle in southern Germany. They are aware of being on the leading edge of something new, something bigger than both of them. They want to get it right. They argue. They disagree. Eventually one of them dips his finger in his beer-froth and writes some words on the table. The other still cannot agree. They go their separate ways, disappointed.

The men are Luther and Zwingli; the year is 1529; the place is Marburg. The dispute is about the presence of Jesus Christ in the Communion, the Eucharist, the Mass.

Both agreed that the Roman Catholic Church had got it wrong with its doctrine of 'transubstantiation'. People often misunderstand this. Within the prevailing philosophy of the Middle Ages, physical objects had outward physical manifestations and an inward 'substance', a reality deeper than that which you could touch and see. So, while the bread still looked, tasted, smelt and felt like bread, its 'substance', this mysterious inner reality, had changed so that it was actually Christ's body.

Luther disagreed, but not by much. He held on to the idea of an inner substance, and said that the substance of Christ's body and the substance of the bread were both present. Zwingli went much further. The bread remained bread and that's all there was to it. At best it could 'signify' Christ's body; it could be a signpost pointing to it, but wouldn't in any sense 'be' the thing itself. Luther's strong point was what Jesus said at the Last Supper: 'This is my body.' He wrote the Latin in beer-froth on the table: *Hoc est corpus meus*. He underlined *est*: this doesn't merely 'signify', it *is* Christ's body. The Lutheran (predominantly German) and the Reformed (predominantly Swiss) Churches have disagreed on the matter ever since.

Meanwhile, less well known than either, a learned man was agonising in the background. Jesus spoke Aramaic, not Latin. Johannes Oecolampadius knew more Hebrew and Aramaic than either Luther or Zwingli. He knew that in Jesus' sentence there wasn't a word for 'is'. Translated literally from Aramaic, Jesus' words were: 'This – my body'. The space represented by that dash between the words is too pregnant for logical analysis. Clearly some deep connection is intended, but you can't put it into a mathematical formula, still less into a test-tube (as some rationalists used to suggest).

Oecolampadius had studied the early Christian theologians who had written on the subject, and had published collections of their sayings. In the early Church there was a range of opinion. What mattered was that those who came to the Lord's

Supper (or whatever you called it) in true faith really did 'feed on Christ'. They really were nourished by the person, the presence and the love of Jesus. How that happened, the theological chemistry of it if you like, wasn't important and probably wasn't knowable either.

The reason for telling you this little bit of church history is quite simple. Oecolampadius, as much as anyone else, influenced what happened in England at the time. John Frith, William Tyndale's assistant, wrote the first book in English on the Lord's Supper while in prison waiting to go to the stake in 1533; he used Oecolampadius's work. Over the next twenty years Thomas Cranmer, the great and tragic Archbishop of Canterbury, did the same, and it is his mature theology, rather than that of Luther or Zwingli, that produced the Book of Common Prayer, thereby influencing countless English-speaking Christians.

Cranmer held on to two things which those who condemned him to die at the stake (1556) could never reconcile. On the one hand, those who came in faith to the Communion really did 'feed on Christ'. On the other hand, the Communion bread remained bread, and did not need to undergo any change. Cranmer never developed a theory of how these things could fit together.

At the same time, however, John Calvin in Geneva was working out a theory not too unlike some thinking in the great Churches of the East. What is really taking place is happening in the heavenly realm. We do not bring Jesus Christ down to our table; by the Spirit, we are taken up into heaven, where Jesus Christ reigns in majesty. The real miracle of the Communion, on this view, is not that anything happens to the bread, but that we are taken into the very heart of heaven, where Christ is at God's right hand.

I find this helpful, but I prefer to think of it in terms of time rather than space. As I have said already, Jesus Christ is the one who comes to us from God's future. His words at the Last Supper mean what they mean within the Passover experience, where bread and wine looked back to the rescue from Egypt and on to the time when Israel would be free at last.

To change the image yet again, Jesus stood in the middle of history, with arms outstretched to past and future, and held them together though it killed him. When we stand at the foot of the cross, when we feast at the table which recalls his final Supper, and when we share at the altar the feast which results from his one and only sacrifice, he is present, feeding us with himself. Remember the grapes of Eshcol.

Remember, too, that when God makes his new world the food will be Jesus himself. That's the meaning of the great discourse in John 6. So what happens when we bring all this together? First, we have food in the present that acts as a symbol of God's future feeding. Second, this is the food over which Jesus said 'my body' and 'my blood'. Third, the Spirit is mysteriously at work in the present to anticipate the life that we will enjoy in God's new world. From these we may conclude that within the whole action of the Holy Communion, the Eucharist – the story, the drama, the actions, and above all the prayer and the love – this food, through the Spirit's mysterious work, is a true anticipation in the present of the food that will sustain us in the age to come. And the name of that food is: Jesus.

13

The greatest drama ever staged (part 1)

One of the best-loved stories in the Bible is the Road to Emmaus (Luke 24:13–35). Cleopas and his companion (probably his wife, Mary) are going home on the evening of the first Easter Day. They are puzzled and sad. A stranger joins them. They tell how their high hopes for Jesus and the redemption of Israel have been dashed by his crucifixion. He explains to them from the scriptures how these things had to be so.

Their excitement grows; they arrive home. They press him to come in. At table, he breaks the bread. Their eyes are opened; they recognise him as Jesus; he vanishes. They run back to Jerusalem to tell the others. The rest, as they say, is history.

The turning-point of the story comes in verse 30: 'As he was reclining with them, he took the bread, blessed it, broke it, and gave it to them.' The words are so close to Luke 22:19, and to the other accounts of the Last Supper (Matthew 26:26; Mark 14:22; 1 Corinthians 11:23–4), that we can be quite sure Luke intended us to 'hear' this part of the story as a strong hint: from now on our hearts will be warmed by the exposition of scripture, and we will know the Lord 'in the breaking of the bread'. The whole story carries the shape, the drama, of the Jesus-meal from that day to this.

And drama it is. Whether in a great cathedral, with choir, organ, robes and processions, or whether on a beach with an upturned Coke crate as table; whether in English or Latin or Swahili or Chinese; whether in sorrow or joy, in gratitude or hope; this drama has been acted out day by day, week by week, by millions of Christians from the very first months of the Church's life to the present. The words are important. But what matters far, far more is the shape and the story. This is indeed a play, the greatest drama ever staged.

Don't be afraid to think of it like that. Indeed, be afraid *not* to think of it like that. It doesn't mean the minister and people are 'play-acting' in some negative sense. This is God's play, and you are privileged to take part in it. You are not at liberty to muck around with the plot. It isn't a service made up of odd bits and pieces tied together with a few hymns and prayers, at the end of which you just happen to share bread and wine. It is God's drama, not yours, rooted in scripture and in the events of which scripture speaks.

The play comes in a rhythm of two parts, within which plenty of variety is possible. First the Word, then the Meal. Scripture is expounded so that the heart is warmed; food is served so that the Lord may be known. You can sit anonymously in church and hear scripture, and a sermon, but you have to receive and eat the bread yourself. We shall look at the first half here, and the second in the next chapter.

The first half of the drama has from quite early times included three sections in particular. Known by their ancient names, they are the *Kyrie*, the *Gloria* and the *Credo*.

Kyrie is the Greek for 'Lord', and is a plea for mercy and help: 'Lord, have mercy; Christ, have mercy; Lord, have mercy.' Into that, whether said or sung, God's people can put all their puzzles and troubles, all their anguish and despair, all their bewilderment and failure and sorrow and sin. They can become Cleopas and Mary on the road, pouring out their troubles to Jesus.

But then, as our hearts begin to trust and hope, we can turn to praise, as we are commanded in all circumstances. So there comes the *Gloria*, 'Glory be to God on high; and on earth peace, goodwill among his people'. It is a shout of praise so emphatic, so exultant, that Thomas Cranmer placed it very near the end of his Communion service, rather than near the beginning, as a 'thank-you' for the whole event. That is just as appropriate. But in ancient liturgies, and most modern ones, it remains near the beginning.

Then there comes the Word itself, the reading and exposition of scripture, always focussed on and climaxing with a Gospel reading. The Old Testament is the start of the story that leads to Jesus, and you can't understand him without it.

The Epistles and Revelation explain his achievement. But the Gospel reading speaks of Jesus himself, his deeds and words, his announcement of the kingdom, his challenge to his contemporaries, his suffering and death, his glorious resurrection. Those who have truly poured out their hearts in the *Kyrie* may well find that this Gospel reading meets them as medicine, comfort and hope.

As our hearts are warmed by the scriptures, so we are stirred up to confess our faith and to pray for the world. The Creed ('We believe in One God . . .') is the badge that Christians wear. It isn't just a list of things we happen to believe in. It states our allegiance to the true God over against all idols, our commitment to know God in Jesus Christ and in the power of the Spirit. It ensures that as we come to the table we are one family. This faith is the single thing that unites the Church as God's people in Christ. And the Prayers then enable us to extend the heartwarming message of the gospel around the world.

The Word of God, said Isaiah, comes down like rain or snow, and does not return to God without accomplishing what he sent it for (Isaiah 55:10–11). When God's Word has had its way with us, then we are ready for the second half of the drama.

14

The greatest drama ever staged (part 2)

'Jesus took bread, blessed it, broke it, and gave it to them.' Four actions heavy with significance. It would still be a Jesus-meal if you did all four in silence, with maybe a single word to refer to Jesus. You could make up some words of your own; some traditions do that (though they tend to sound rather the same as they did last time). But, just as a wedding couple will choose a gold ring, if they can afford it, rather than a plastic one, so the Church down the years has chosen special words, choice phrases, to approach the central mystery, God's gift of his own very self in the person of his Son, in words that at least try to do justice to the reality. Liturgy at this point is like good orchestration for wonderful music; just as you don't play a Beethoven symphony on a mouth-organ, so you will not want to celebrate the Jesus-meal casually or flippantly. The best demands the best.

Somewhere around the transition from Word to Sacrament there may be opportunity for the confession and absolution of sin. Sometimes this is done at the very beginning of the service instead. There are good arguments for either, but it must happen in one place or the other. 'One should examine oneself,' said Paul, 'and then eat the bread and drink the cup.' Many traditions have encouraged Christians to prepare carefully for this meal. If you were invited to dinner with royalty, you would think some days in advance what you were going to wear. What about when you're invited to supper with the Lord of the world?

Then comes the first of the four actions: taking the bread. This can be done very simply; or it can be dramatic, with members of the congregation bringing the bread and wine (sometimes called the 'elements', the basic parts of the drama) to the front. Unlike some pagan worship, the symbols of the Jesus-meal are not grain and grapes, but bread and wine: fruit of the earth, fruit of the vine, *and* the work of human hands. We did not initiate this action; God did. But now, in grateful obedience, we bring these tokens of our own life and work, laying ourselves before God as we do so in readiness for his will.

The second of the actions is the blessing. Some worry about whether we can or should 'bless' material objects. Isn't that a form of magic? Emphatically not. If Jesus blessed the bread, so can we. To bless it is to pray that it may become, within the rhythm and drama of the whole event, the vessel and vehicle of God's Jesus-shaped love for each recipient and so for the world. God's good creation, longing for its own redemption, is taken up into the saving purposes of God, with past and future rushing together into the present moment. So the celebrant or president greets the people in the Lord's name, and instructs them to 'Lift up your hearts!' and they respond, 'We lift them up to the Lord.' We come into Jesus' presence. As at Emmaus, those who thought they were inviting him to supper discovered that he was the host, and they the guests.

The 'blessing' often takes the form of a long prayer, in which the saving acts of God are set out and celebrated, reaching their climax with Jesus' life, death and resurrection. The celebration bursts out in the *Sanctus*, the hymn of praise the angels sang in Isaiah 6, the song of the living creatures in Revelation 4: 'Holy, holy, holy, Lord God of hosts'. Singing this, the Church is fulfilling its central vocation, summing up the praises of the whole created order, from antelopes to archangels.

Then, or slightly later, another hymn can be said or sung, the *Benedictus qui venit*: 'Blessed is he who comes in the name of the Lord!' This phrase, taken from Matthew 23:39, is a Jewish way of saying 'welcome'. This greeting has sometimes been linked to the Roman doctrine of the 'real presence' of Christ, via transubstantiation (see Chapter 12); but it is just as appropriate within other views of Jesus' presence to and with the worshippers and the elements.

Then the third action: the bread is broken. The symbolism, linking the bread to the whole story of Jesus, climaxing in his death, is too powerful for words, and too all-embracing to capture in any neat theological formula. Suffice it to say that this is the symbol Jesus himself gave us as his way for us to be enfolded within the meaning of his own death. He didn't give us a theory, he gave us an action, and this is it. Do it in remembrance of him. And be in awe.

Then, at some stage, the prayer which Jesus himself taught us. Some liturgies put it just before receiving Communion, some just after. Either way, it belongs closely here, not least but not only because of its prayer for daily bread and for forgiveness of sins. This is the Christian family meal, and we rightly say, 'Our Father . . .'

And then the moment. Jesus took, blessed, broke . . . and gave. We come; we receive. Like all truly joyful things, this one is also solemn, too deep for shallow or casual happiness. Like all truly solemn moments, this one can carry more joy than most. Of course, whether or not you 'feel' anything special at the time depends on a million things to do with your life, your health, the weather, the time of the year and the month, and so on. But from the earliest days of the Church this has been one of the central means whereby Christians have been nourished in faith, hope and love. And, in keeping with the solemnity, the ancient hymn may be said or sung, known as the *Agnus Dei*: 'Lamb of God, you take away the sins of the world; have mercy upon us. Grant us peace.'

The drama has reached its climax. Silence is appropriate. A wise friend once told me he always went back to his seat and re-read the Gospel passage, listening for whatever God might want to whisper to him in the intimacy of the moment. It is a moment of commitment, dedication, peace, love. Enjoy it. Then, usually a bit too soon, we sing a hymn or say a prayer, and are dismissed. We have already received the greatest possible blessing, and to be 'blessed' again is not necessary, though many still appreciate it. The important thing is that, like Cleopas and Mary, we are sent out as witnesses, into all the world, as rejuvenated, nourished Christians, 'to live and work to God's praise and glory'. The Church's mission is an essential part of the drama of the Jesus-meal.

15

Table manners and table matters

There is much more that could be said. This little book is only a short introduction to a huge subject. But I want, in concluding, to look at six obvious questions.

First, *Why*? Why do we do this? In a sense, the whole book has been an attempt to answer this question. But it may help to look at two wrong answers. The first is the grudging 'because Jesus told us to'. That's true, and important. But it can imply that there can be no other good reason, and often goes with a view of God's created world, and the sacramental life in general, that is dualistic, believing that to have any serious dealings with creation, let alone to bring it into the Christian life, is dangerous. The only answer I can give to that is that it's far, far more dangerous not to.

The second wrong answer (though no-one would actually come out and say this) is that by celebrating the Jesus-meal we are earning favour with God. We are manipulating God and creation so that things work out well for us. No doubt some have tried to use this symbol, and lots of others, that way. It doesn't work, but that's not what matters; to approach the sacrament like that is to miss the point altogether. Why then? Because this meal makes sense of the rest of the cosmos, of Jesus, of the Spirit, of our human nature, of who the creator/redeemer God is. That's why.

Second, *When*? The Jews keep Passover once a year. There are some churches, notably the Free Church of Scotland, who have Communion once a year, and a very solemn, holy and memorable occasion it is too. I'd much rather that than a casual or flippant 'whenever I suddenly feel like it' approach. However, the early Church seems to have celebrated the Lord's Supper on a much more regular basis: at least once a week, and perhaps in some quarters more, too. A few centuries ago, church leaders, including the great reformers, struggled to persuade people, even very devout people, to receive Communion on a weekly basis. The culture of the times was against it. Now many people receive Communion not just each Sunday but often during the week as well. When I was engaged in regular pastoral ministry I found that the only way I could cope with the daily demands was the daily Eucharist. There I could lay all my puzzles and problems symbolically before God and find them not removed but reshaped in the pattern of Jesus.

Beyond that the best rule is to work out a model that stretches you a little, that meets your needs but also challenges you to a deeper commitment. Not simply 'what I feel comfortable with'; who said you should always feel comfortable at table with the Lord of the world? No: the pattern that has the mark of discipleship on it for where you are right now.

Third, *What?* When all is said and done, what is going on in this service? The answer is that the whole world is coming, symbolically in that bread and wine, to the foot of the cross. The Church is a 'royal priesthood', gathering up the praises and pains of creation and turning them into prayer and sacrament. And this must mean that justice and peace are flowing out from the Eucharist as well. When Paul says that, in celebrating this meal, we 'announce the death of the Lord until he comes', he doesn't mean that it's a good opportunity for preaching. He means that *the action itself*, the Jesus-drama, the thing Jesus told us to do, announces to the principalities and powers, the unseen forces in the world, that Jesus is Lord, and that his cross has won the victory over all evil. And the Church, cheered and encouraged by that, can go out to put that victory into practice, in the City Council, in the classroom, in the unemployment bureau, the cancer ward, the peace negotiations.

Fourth, *Where?* Anywhere at all. But the choice of location must not be frivolous. If the Eucharist does indeed announce to the principalities and powers that Jesus has won the victory over them on the cross, then from time to time one may need to celebrate the Jesus-meal right on their front doorstep: on the runway where a nuclear bomber is trying to take off, on the street outside the headquarters of a terrorist organisation, in a school playground after a tragic accident. Many hospitals have chapels, and many will allow a Communion service to be held on a ward when appropriate.

But all that is like saying that you can drink a good wine out of anything at all; the wine is more important than the glass, and, if all you've got is a plastic cup, that will do. But normally, just as you want to drink good wine from the right sort of glass, you will want to celebrate the Jesus-meal in a place built specially for the purpose: yes, a church. There, within walls that have the prayers of generations soaked into them, with rafters that have rung before with the praises of humans and (who knows?) angels, the resonances should be right. There is such a thing as what one might call a 'spiritual acoustic'; some buildings will resonate well spiritually with the Jesus-meal, and many of those buildings will be churches.

Fifth, *How?* With joy and dignity. Getting the balance between those two is always a matter of fine judgment, and will relate quite closely to the culture(s) where the meal is taking place. Joy can turn into flippancy, dignity into stuffiness. Watch out for both.

Within that, it is my considered judgment, after over twenty years of celebrating the Jesus-meal in churches, chapels, cathedrals, hospitals, students' rooms, hotels, in ancient ruins, on hillsides and beaches (including, once, under the puzzled eye of a Turkish soldier, on the beach where Paul said goodbye to the Ephesian elders) that if the leader(s) know the shape of the service (the Emmaus shape we looked at in the previous chapters), and if they are sensitive to the people they are with and the traditions they come from, there are all sorts of variations, moments of freedom within the structure, which can be built in. Equally, there are all sorts of times when one must stick to the structure for all its worth, for the spiritual health of all concerned. This is always going to be a matter of personal, Spirit-led judgment.

Under this rubric I include the question of whether or not to wear particular robes; whether or not to use particular postures (to kneel at certain points, for instance); whether or not to use incense, bells and indeed music; how much to involve the congregation with parts of the service; whether or not to use what are called 'manual acts' (crossing yourself, lifting up the bread in thanksgiving, and so on). I know that most of these things have been given varied theological 'meanings', and that some people, to avoid the meaning, have avoided the action. Read Romans 14 and 1 Corinthians 8: those who have tender consciences are to be respected. But Paul always aimed not only to respect, but to educate. Those entrusted with ministry in a church should have that double aim too.

Finally, *Who?* It is tempting to say 'Anyone at all!' and indeed some recent writers, impressed with the way the Jesus-meal picks up where Jesus' regular free-for-all parties left off, have urged us to see the Communion service as the place where a warm welcome is extended to all who want to come within range of the love of God in Jesus, whether or not they are ready for a signed-up commitment. From very early on, though, that was not the Church's policy and practice. This was partly, no doubt, because there was political danger in being found out by someone who didn't belong. It was also partly because of the special intimacy of Communion, which didn't and often doesn't seem appropriate for someone who doesn't yet know Jesus at all. That, I know, could be argued either way. But most churches have some kind of basic rule of membership: baptism, or baptism and confirmation, are normal.

On one matter of current debate I think we must hold the traditional line very firmly. The Eucharist, Communion, the Jesus-meal, is not the possession of a set of private groups. It is God's gift to the people of God in Christ as a whole. It is vital that the person presiding should be in some way a sign of that unity, through being accredited with the wider body of the Church. It won't do for anyone at all to pop up and preside. In most churches this means some form of ordination. Just now there is a move in some quarters, not least as a long-delayed reaction to a now almost non-existent 'priestcraft', to show just how little we care for 'priests' by saying that in principle anyone, lay or ordained, can preside. That scores one point at the cost of missing a dozen others. This meal is a vital symbol of our unity. Don't let's use it to play party games.

However, on another point I think the tradition needs changing. I would plead strongly with those churches that have not yet done so to regard *all* the baptised, including children, as rightful recipients of Communion. Linking confirmation to Communion was a mediaeval trick to boost the numbers of confirmation candidates. Baptism is the way into the family; the Eucharist is the family meal. Of course, babies need to learn table manners before they can take regular part. But I see no justification for keeping Communion as an adults-only event. At a Jewish Passover the youngest child present has a speaking part, asking, 'Why is this night different from all other nights?' There are special things for the children to do as part of the celebration. I look forward to the day in my own church when the liturgy will include the youngest child present asking, 'Why is this meal different from all other meals?' – and getting a good answer.

Another plea to end with. From the first generation of the Church, eating together was a sign of the breaking down of boundaries between Christians of different groups: Jew and Greek (Galatians 2), rich and poor (1 Corinthians 11), and so on. This was a sign of God's saving justice going out into all the world. When this caused difficulties, Paul was adamant, in the name of the Jesus who had included everyone at his table, that unity there was not negotiable. 'We, who are many, are one bread, one body – for we all partake of the one bread' (1 Corinthians 10:17). Sharing Communion together between Christians of different denominations ought not to be the goal at the end of a long process of unity negotiations. It ought to be the means, the thing we already do, that will create a context in which we will be able to understand and respect one another, and grow towards a richer unity. I know not everybody will agree with this. But I'm pretty sure St Paul would have done.

Go in peace, to love and serve the Lord!
In the name of Christ – Amen!